THE HISTORY OF THE MAGNA CARTA

A BRIEF HISTORY WITH THE ORIGINAL MAGNA CARTA

JAMES K WHEATON

GOLGOTHA PRESS, INC.

CONTENTS

1

INTRODUCTION

The simplest definition of the Magna Carta is that it was a charter, originally signed between King John of England and his barons that granted those barons certain liberties and political rights. Yet the document is so much more than just that. The Magna Carta (a Latin phrase which translates in English to "Great Charter") came to be seen as one of the most important documents in all of Western civilization.

Its significance, both its actual and practical implications as well as it's perceived and imagined ones, influenced the common man's struggle against monarchial rule. It had a tremendous influence on the set-up of the legal system of England, and, as the empire of England expanded, became the basis for many governments in the Western Hemisphere. The Magna Carta was the foundation for many of the democracies that would be born over the years--especially those that trace their origins to the English Crown.

THE ORIGINS OF THE MAGNA CARTA

The origins of the Magna Carta deal with an inept King, territories in France, a dispute with the Pope, no clear successor for an unpopular leader, and the set-up of the English feudal system. All of this came to a head in the year 1215.

To understand the Magna Carta, it is first important to understand feudal England. Feudal society required that the barons held their land in fee from the King. As such, they pledged an oath of loyalty and obedience to him. While the King of England could be considered "all-powerful," the truth was that his power was reliant on the barons of his land. It was the barons who supplied the King with the troops he needed whenever war came, and it was the barons who would collect the taxes to fund the King's expenses--both foreign and domestic. In both instances, it was expected that the King would consult with the barons prior towards taking any action. When kings were successful, especially in their military campaigns, the system would work. Military failure, however, could spell doom.

AT THE BEGINNING of the 13th century, England possessed territory in France (captured during the many wars England and France fought throughout the years). King John, however, was unable to hold this land. By 1204, he had lost most of the English-held territories in northern France. To gain them back, King John continued a campaign on French soil. He raised taxes without the barons' consent and demanded even more troops of them.

King John also had issues with the papacy. A 1207 quarrel over the next Archbishop of Canterbury excommunicated King John and made all christening and marriages in England illegal under Church law. Medieval England, very much under the sway of the papacy and very fearful of being doomed to hell, was extremely worried at these occurrences and blamed John for their possible afterlife, which they believed would be spent in hell. While King John finally relented to the Pope's wishes in 1214, the damage to his reputation had already been done. By 1215, the complete defamation of his character would be complete.

It began in 1214, on foreign soil. In that year, King John suffered defeat yet again in Northern France, and responded again with demands of higher taxes and more men of his barons. The barons, though, would have no more of King John's demands and rebelled against him. The rebellion itself was not unique (every king since William the Conqueror had faced some sort of rebellion); the fact that there was no obvious replacement for John was. Prior rebellions had rallied around this potential replacement. This rebellion would have to be different. Instead of seeking a replacement, it would have to seek something else.

The barons captured London but could not completely defeat John, so in 1215, both sides met to discuss the matter. The result of that piece that was procured became known as the Magna Carta.

THE MAGNA CARTA 1215

The main focus of the Magna Carta dealt with curbing abuses of the feudal system (in fact, about two thirds of the document dealt with these abuses). The barons wrote the Magna Carta, which contained 63 clauses promising all freemen access to courts and a fair trial, eliminating unfair fines and punishments, giving power to the Catholic Church in England, and addressing many lesser issues. As the rebellion was due to several barons coming together, certain clauses can be seen as concessions to one or two barons in particular, especially those that dealt with everything from royal forests, debts to removal of fish weirs.

The truly radical part of the document, though, was the concept of what we would later call (in our own Declaration of Independence) the concept of unalienable rights. The barons sought to clarify that there were certain rights that no King could infringe upon. This was truly a revolutionary idea. It claimed that as an English baron, they had rights that were universal, that had to be applied and that could not be interpreted as a king saw fit. It showed that the King was bound to the law, that there were certain laws that were bigger than the King.

The document also included a way to enforce the rules that the Magna Carta held. This was contained in clause 61, a check against the King. The clause established a committee of 25 barons who could overrule the King if he defied the Magna Carta, inclusive of taking back land and possessions of the King himself.

The Magna Carta was written by Archbishop Stephen Langston (though others involved included Eleanor of Aquataine, King Henry II, Richard of Clare, Gilbert de Clare, Richard the Lionheart /Richard I, and Edward Coke). The King affixed his great seal to the document (which was originally known as the Articles of the Barons) on June 15, 1215 in the meadow at Runnymede. In response, the barons renewed their oath to the King. Copies of the document were soon distributed throughout England.

ENGLISH HISTORY AFTER THE ORIGINAL MAGNA CARTA

King John began defying the document almost immediately after it was signed (or rather sealed, as it is unknown if John had the ability to write). One particular problem was clause 61, which was a severe, and potential lethal challenge, to the King's authority as a monarch. In this, the Pope agreed, as Pope Innocent III annulled the document (seeing clause 61 as a problem of the papal's authority over the King). Realizing that the King would not be restrained by the Magna Carta, the barons rebelled again. England was embroiled in a civil war, known as the First Baron's War. The barons attempted to replace King John (at one point offering the crown of England to the King of France).

Had this been the end of the story, the Magna Carta may have become forgotten in history, a document that had failed in its attempt to avert a war between the King and the barons and having a life of validity that lasted only a few short months. It was the death of King John in 1216, and political maneuvering by is replacements, however, that ensured the Magna Carta's legacy.

CHARTER OF 1216

Despite the death of King John, the barons continued their war against the crown. King John's replacement (his son King Henry III) was only nine years old at the time, so in his place Guala Bicchieri ruled the country (as a papal legate, a sort of legal guardian for the King). As the war was being fought because of the rejection of the Magna Carta, (and the clauses that went along with it) Bicchieri (and loyalists to the King led by William Marshall) executed a daft political move. To undercut the barons and their reasoning for the war, they reissued the Charter of Liberties.

The Charter of 1216 was nothing more than a reissue of the original Great Charter (the first Magna Carta). It was issued in the King's name on

November 12, 1216 as a Royal concession to the rebels. It was a political document, a power move by the King's men in an effort to remain in power. It is important to note, however, that it was not a verbatim reissuance of the Great Charter of 1215. There were several notable differences, and these differences dealt more with what was taken out than anything that was added.

Whereas the original Great Charter had 61 clauses, the Charter of 1216 was reduced to 42. Most notably, article 61 was removed. Clause 61 established the committee of 25 barons to oversee and, in the case of Kingly violations, overrule the crown if the King did not comply with the charter.

Other clauses that limited the powers of the King were also deleted. Clauses 12 and 14, which required the King to receive approval of a common council of the realm before levying taxes, were taken out. The clauses that dealt with debt and taxes (Clauses 25 and 26), as well as the one that dealt with intestacy (instances where someone died without having made out a will), were also deleted. Subjects were no longer allowed to leave the kingdom without their allegiance coming under question (as it had with Clause 42 of the original). The King was given free range to appoint justices, constables, sheriffs and bailiffs (a year earlier it was required that such positions only go to those who knew the law and would uphold it).

Evil customs associated with the forests were no longer abolished (clause 48 of the original). Restrictions on royal officers were removed, as was the requirement that all foreign knights and mercenaries to leave the realm. Hostage returns, part of the original Great Charter of 1215, were not found in the 1216 version.

It is important to remember why these differences occurred. In 1215, a Great Charter was being forced onto the King. In 1216, it was the crown that was creating the charter. It kept clauses that the King (and at this time, it really was his guardians, as the King was too young to partake in its drafting) could, in a sense, live with while removing those clauses that limited the crown's power. The Charter was also issued separately for Ireland.

CHARTER OF 1217

The end of the First Barons War, and the treaty that followed it, led to yet another reissuance of the Magna Carta. Again there were amendments made, and again there was a separate charter issued for Ireland.

The Charter of 1216 had 42 clauses; the one of 1217 was expanded to 47.

The significance of the Charter of 1217 is twofold. It is in this charter that we first get the name Magna Carta, which would be applied to all previous charters, and all future ones. More significantly, however, is the issuance of a complementary Charter, known as the Charter of the Forest, that would go hand in hand with the Magna Carta from here on out.

The original Magna Carta, and its many incarnations and reissues, dealt with the rights of the barons. In the Charter of 1217, and specifically the Charter of the Forest, rights and privileges for the common man were sought. The protection of these rights, while they only applied to behavior in the King's forest, were the first time that the common man was considered in any legal document.

To understand why the Charter of the Forest is significant, it is important to understand what the forest meant to medieval England. In this time period, a forest was not what we think of today (a collection of trees) but instead applied to meadows and fields, as well as forested land. But more than that, it was where the common man of England found wood to heat his home, firewood to cook his meals. Charcoal was taken from the forest and used in certain businesses and trades. Food could be foraged there, and animals could be hunted there. Farmers could allow their livestock to graze in the forests.

Under the Charter of the Forest, penalties against the commoners were reduced for infractions in forested land. Mutilation and the death penalty were abolished for the stealing of venison.

The Charter of the Forest was actually a step back in time, restoring the traditional rights of the citizens of England. The land had once been seen as common for all, and the Charter of the Forest sought to bring back that sense of community. It applied to free men only (which covered only 1of the total population, as many English citizens were, in fact, serfs tied to the land and particularly that land's owner). Such access by the common man to royal lands would wait almost 500 years, until England joined with Scotland in 1707, to see it equaled.

Amazingly, this law stayed on the books for centuries. From its issuance, it was the law of the land until 1971, when it was superseded by the Wild Creatures and Forest Laws Act 1971.

7

THE CHARTER OF 1225

In 1225, King Henry III (King John's son) reached the age of eighteen, which made him an adult (the age of majority in England). As such, he was firmly in control of his country and was asked to confirm the Charters of 1216 and 1217.

Again, as in 1217, there was some politically maneuvering. The Charter of 1225 included a statement explaining that the Charter was done of the King's own free will, an attempt to show that it was not forced upon him but instead could be considered his idea. Since it was an issuance from the King, it included changes to the Charters of 1216 and 1217.

This new Magna Carta had only 37 clauses (as compared with the 47 clauses of the Charter of 1217). Regulations on feudal relief (what we would call today an inheritance tax) were removed from the new Charter, as were regulations forbidding the overexploitation of a ward's property by his guardian. A guardian could now force his ward to marry a partner of lower social standing (commonly done to receive a higher dowry). Widows could no longer be expected to receive their dowry and inheritance promptly (and some would find they would not receive them at all), and could be compelled to remarry (the Charter of 1217 had protected them from such actions).

Debtors also did not fare well with the new charter. In the Charter of 1217, debtors would not have their land seized if they had a debt but had other means to pay it off. The Charter of 1225 has no mention of this.

The new charter did have some notable additions. The new clauses mainly concerned land. Free men, for instance, could not give away or sell their land if doing so meant that they could not meet their feudal obligations to their lord. Free men could also not give their land to a religious house and then receive it back again. As these clauses show, the Magna Carta was evolving with the times, addressing issues that were coming up during the course of events (it is also important to note that these clauses further strengthened the lords owner-ship on the "free men" that were attached to their land).

Again, it is important to see that the Charter of 1225 was issued by the King and was not something that was forced upon him. The Charter of 1225 was done, as it was stated in the Charter itself, of the King's own free will. As such, as is the case with the Charter of 1216, certain items were removed from previous charters that could be seen as a hindrance, either to the King or to those in positions of authority.

It is important to note too that the Charter of 1225 does not repudiate the Charter of the Forest. The rights of the common man (and really, the free men of England) were still protected.

While not part of the Charter of 1225, a declara-tion by the King in 1227 was yet another sign of the reconfirmation of the King's power. In 1227, Henry III declared that only edicts and charters bearing his own seal were legal. This questioned the validity of previous Charters (specifically the Charter of 1217, which was not done by his hand). It took an edict from the King (a carta parva issued in 1237) to confirm all previous charters and to grant them in perpetuity.

THE GREAT CHARTER 1297: STATUTE

The Charter of 1297 was a situation of history repeating itself. Edward I was yet another English King involved in yet another campaign overseas (this time in Flanders, a geographical region located in parts of present-day Belgium, France, and the Netherlands). Again money was needed to finance the campaign. Again, the King faced an issue with the church. Pope Boniface VIII had just issued edicts that forbid his clergy to pay taxes to a secular ruler. As such, Edward was having trouble financing his Flanders' campaign.

To raise the funds, Edward applied a tax on English wool. He also forced the barons to grant him aid. This angered the barons, who again raised arms against their king. So again, the Magna Carta became a political instrument, a move by a King to undercut his armed (and angry) nobility.

To forestall a possible revolution and civil war, Edward reconfirmed the various charters of his predecessors, which the previous Magna Cartas touched on before. This Confirmation of Charters was in many ways similar to the parva carta issued in 1237 by King Henry III.

The Confirmation reinforced the principle of no taxation without consent (to America this would be changed to the more memorable "No taxation without representation" in her revolution). It also laid down the fact that the various clauses of the Magna Carta were to apply to all freemen (and for the Charter of the Forest to all common men) and that they were to be upheld by those who uphold the laws and administer justice in the land. Sheriffs, shires, and officers were specifically named to ensure that they continued to administer justice according to the Magna Carta.

It also placed no time limit on the Magna Carta. The clauses and agreements of the Magna Carta were not only to apply to the current generation of nobility and freemen but also their heirs. The same applied to those asked to the King's officers and nobility and those charged with upholding and administering the law. Their heirs, and those who replaced them, were required to adhere to its clauses. In exchange for these concessions, the nobility agreed to the tax hike.

Politically, this was a concession of the King for a greater purpose (as far as the King was concerned). The King reconfirmed the Magna Carta in exchange for tax money. Constitutionally, though, this can be seen as the most important of all the Magna Cartas. It is because this confirmation made the Magna Carta statute. It was no longer an agreement between the nobility and the King; it became bigger than a King, a generation, a group of people. It was not an agreement for their time but a set of laws for all time. No longer would barons or the common man need to fret about their rights (though as we shall see, they continued to do so). No longer would Magna Cartas need to be issued. It became the law of the land, and would remain so for hundreds of years.

LATER HISTORY OF THE CHARTER

The Six Statutes

A s with any legal document, certain clarifications needed to be made, especially as differing circumstances came to confront the citizens of England and its King. Between 1331 and 1369 King Edward III passed six measures (known as the Six Statutes) that sought such clarifications.

Important amongst these explanations was the declaration that the Magna Carta was the supreme law of the land. Statutes that ran contrary to something in the Magna Carta were to be abolished, that the Magna Carta superseded all other statutes. In addition, Edward helped to better define those who the Magna Carta applied to. Instead of it being free men, itself a definition that was perhaps hard to pin down, the Magna Carta would apply to all men throughout the kingdom, regardless of their position or lot in life.

The Statutes of Edward III also introduced the concept of due process of law. It guaranteed that the citizens of England would not face prison or death, or forfeiture of land or property, without having their day in court. They were to be judged by their peers and be held to the laws of the land.

Reconfirmation of the Charter

Despite the various edicts and differing versions of the Magna Carta (especially the one of 1297, which promised that the clauses would be applied across generations) the people of England were always concerned that the King, whomever it may be at the time, might not follow the rules of the Magna Carta. As such, each generation of English citizens sought their King to reconfirm the charter (with the goal of such a reconfirmation that the King would also abide by the Magna Carta). Over two centuries, this led to the Magna Carta being reconfirmed between

32 and 45 times. It was last confirmed in 1423 by King Henry VI.

Tudor Period

By the mid 1400s, the Magna Carta was not seen as an important document, due to the rise of Parliament (itself a check and balance against the King). Newly passed statutes, based in part on the Magna Carta, also held more sway.

In fact, it took misinterpretations of the Magna Carta to cause further changes in English political life. Clause 39 of the original charter, for instance, became the claim for a jury system and trials for the English citizens. Puritans began to believe the Magna Carta as a statement of their liberties (the concept of inalienable rights, or rights that were above government control).

17th and 18th Centuries

The Magna Carta continued to be interpreted, and misinterpreted, by differing English groups throughout the years, to best serve their individual needs and beliefs. Habeas corpus was linked to the

Magna Carta in a court case. Groups sought to establish laws based on the Magna Carta, and refusal to do so led to armies being raised (in 1642-49 and again in 1689).

Radical groups would either support or tear down the Magna Carta as they saw fit. Levellers rejected it as they believed it to be 'Norman.' Magna Carta was seen as less free than what Englanders had enjoyed prior to the Norman invasions. Others saw it as a statement of liberties, and any time their liberties were infringed upon (radicals like Richard Overton and Gerrard Winstanley) they called out the Magna Carta's name.

In time more logical interpretations began to emerge about the Magna Carta. It came to be seen as more of a social contract, an agreement between government and its people (in the line of John Locke's social contract). The Magna Carta came to be seen as the foundation of the English constitution.

In America, the charters for the colonies would directly or indirectly reference the Magna Carta. Copies of the Magna Carta were distributed to the colonists. In other British sovereigns, the Magna Carta would spring up, again as the basis of the laws for that area. As we will see, later when those lands received their independence from England they based much of their constitutions, as well as the laws that governed them, on the Magna Carta.

Repeal of Articles of the Charter

For many, many generations, the Magna Carta was held to be one of the greatest documents in the land (which would have surprised many who had initially worked on it, as they did not believe themselves to be drafting anything too radical or history changing). It became a symbol for the citizens of England (referenced by those in the English Civil War as proof that the King was bound by law). It became a reference point for revolutions (inclusive of our own American one).

As such, there was always hesitation to repeal or change any part of the Magna Carta. Doing so, it could be seen, was to show that the document was not as important as it needed to be (if one part were seen as fallible, then other parts could be as well. The English citizens always feared that the King would reassert his power, which is why they asked for continued reconfirmations of the Magna Carta and why they did not seek to change parts of it).

In 1828, in an effort to consolidate certain criminal laws, the Magna Carta finally faced the possibility of change. The Lord Lansdowne's Act by the English Parliament dealt with offences against the person, inclusive of violence. The intent was clarity and simplicity, as the act combined a number of earlier statutes into a single Act. One of the Statutes it clarified (and in doing so replaced) was Clause 26 of the Magna Carta. This represented the first time any part of the Magna Carta was repealed. It would not, however, be the last.

With the repeal of one of the clauses, the invincibility and unchanging nature of the document was gone. The sacredness of the clauses was broken. The time for change had come. Over the next 140 years, the charter was broken down, and major parts of it were repealed (it is important to note that the clauses were simply replaced by differing and updated Statutes. The King did not regain the powers he lost at the signing of the first version of the Magna Carta). In fact, a majority of the clauses were repealed in two acts. The Statute Law Revision Act of 1863 repealed most of the clauses that applied in England and Wales. In 1872, Ireland followed suit, with its own Statute Law Revision Act.

The 20th century saw the repeal of more than 10 of the statutes. All in all, after 1969, only three clauses remained in effect. These clauses were 1, 9 and 29.

CLAUSES STILL IN EFFECT TODAY

Amazingly, three clauses of the 1297 Magna Carta are still in effect today. Or perhaps, after looking at them, it becomes evident why they are still in effect. One addresses one of the problems that led to the drafting of the original Magna Carta Charter in 1215; the second protects the ancient liberties of a powerful city; and the final has become the basis of English law.

Clause 1, the freedom of the English Church

This clause grants the freedom of the English Church. It can be seen as a separation of church and state, whereby the state is not to interfere with the rights and liberties of the Church.

Clause 9, the "ancient liberties" of the City of London

This clause grants the ancient liberties of the City of London. One of the more important provisions of these ancient liberties was the right of London's citizens to elect their own mayor.

Clause 29, the Right to Do Process

This is the basis of the entire legal system, both in England and America. It protects the rights and freedom of a country's citizens. Citizens will not be imprisoned, or be denied land, liberty; they will not be outlawed or exiled, unless they break the laws of the land, or by judgment of his peers. This is the backbone of common law, notably the concept of trial by jury. It states, in no uncertain terms, that a citizen has certain rights that are neither arbitrary nor capricious.

THE IMPORTANCE OF THE MAGNA CARTA

The Magna Carta can be considered a turning point in the way governments governed. Up until this point, the law of the land and the word of the king were one and the same. Rights seemingly emanated from the King. The system did more than simply imbue the King with "god-like" powers; it determined that a country's citizens were literally the King's subjects, subject to his beliefs and fancies.

The Magna Carta changed all this, though not at first and not for all English citizens. By signing the document (or rather affixing his seal to it), King John placed himself and all future rulers to rule within the law. Barons (and other free-men of the monarchy) were granted rights that no King could take away. Free-men (and it is important to remember that this distinction did not include serfs) were not subject to arbitrarily rules. There were a specific set of laws that now governed them. It seems rudimentary now, because the concept has become so ingrained within our society. Yet this was revolutionary at the time.

It is for this precise reason that it is so common, that the Magna Carta is so important to us now. The Magna Carta is more than the precursor to modern British law, the US Constitution and its Bill of Rights. It became the backbone of the laws throughout the English-speaking world. When the English expanded into the New World, they brought with them the tenants of the Magna Carta. The American Revolution was as much about preserving the liberties guaranteed them in the Magna Carta, as it was fighting for a new country.

This is clear in our country's constitution. Look no further than the fifth amendment, which guarantees that no citizen shall be "deprived life, liberty, or property, without due process of law," and see how it mimics the Magna Carta, which states that "No freeman shall be taken, imprisoned...except by the lawful judgment of his peers, or by the law of the land."

The Magna Carta was an important step in the history of democracy. It established limits on a monarchy, which set the stage for future concessions from royalty. It really beefed up the concept of private property, while establishing the belief of equal application of the law throughout the land. A process was established to settle disputes (mostly of property).

The Magna Carta understood that laws needed to be bigger than the person enforcing them, that they needed to be universal to the citizens of a land. Laws could not fall to the interpretation of a single person but needed to be upheld for generations. Free men needed to be granted certain rights that no one, not even the King, could take away. It was in this belief that the Magna Carta was born.

THE ORIGINAL MAGNA CARTA
(TRANSLATED FROM LATIN)

J ohn, by the grace of God, king of England,
lord of Ireland, duke of Normandy and
Aquitaine, and count of Anjou, to the archbishops, bishops, abbots, earls,barons, justiciars, foresters, sheriffs, stewards, servants, and to all
his bailiffs and liege subjects, greeting. Know that,
having regard to God and for the salvation of our
soul, and those of all our ancestors and heirs, and
unto the honor of God and the advancement of holy
church, and for the reform of our realm, by advice of
our venerable fathers, Stephen archbishop of
Canterbury, primate of all England and cardinal of
the holy Roman Church, Henry archbishop of
Dublin, William of London, Peter of Winchester,
Jocelyn of Bath and Glastonbury, Hugh of Lincoln,

Walter of Worcester, William of Coventry, Benedict of Rochester, bishops; of master Pandulf, subdeacon and member of the household of our lord the Pope, of brother Aymeric (master of the Knights of the Temple in England), and of the illustrious men William Marshall earl of Pembroke, William earl of Salisbury, William earl of Warenne, William earl ofArundel, Alan of Galloway (constable of Scotland), Waren Fitz Gerald, Peter Fits Herbert, Hubert de Burgh (seneschal of Poitou), Hugh de Neville, Matthew Fitz Herbert, Thomas Basset, Alan Basset, Philip d'Aubigny, Robert of Roppesley, John Marshall, John Fitz Hugh, and others, our liegemen.

I. In the first place we have granted to God, and by this our present charter confirmed for us and our heirs for ever that the English church shall be free, and shall have her rights entire, and her liberties inviolate; and we will that it be thus observed; which is apparent from this that the freedom of elections, which is reckoned most important and very essential to the English church, we, of our pure and uncon-strained will, did grant, and did by our charter confirm and did obtain the ratification of the same from our lord, Pope Innocent III., before the quarrel arose between us and our barons: and this we will observe, and our will is that it be observed in good faith by our heirs for ever. We have also granted to all freemen of our kingdom, for us and our heirs for ever, all the underwritten liberties, to be had and held by them and their heirs, of us and our heirs for ever.

2. If any of our earls or barons, or others holding of us in chief by military service shall have died, and at the time of his death his heir shall be of full age and owe "relief" he shall have his inheritance on payment of the ancient relief, namely the heir or heirs of an earl, 100 pounds for a whole earl's barony; the heir or heirs of a baron, 100 pounds for a whole barony; the heir or heirs of a knight, 100 shillings at most for a whole knight's fee; and whoever owes less let him give less, according to the ancient custom of fiefs.

3. If, however, the heir of any of the aforesaid has been under age and in wardship, let him have his inheritance without relief and without fine when hecomes of age.

4. The guardian of the land of an heir who is thus under age, shall take from the land of the heir nothing but reasonably produce, reasonable customs, and reasonable services, and that without destruction or waste of men or goods; and if we have committed the wardship of the lands of any such

minor to the sheriff, or to any other who is respon-
sible to us for its issues, and he has made destruction or waste of what he holds in wardship, we will
take of him amends, and the land shall be
committed to two lawful and discreet men of that
fee, who shall be responsible for the issues to us or
to him to whom we shall assign them; and if we have
given or sold the wardship of any such land to
anyone and he has therein made destruction or
waste, he shall lose that wardship,and it shall be
transferred to two lawful and discreet men of that
fief, who shall be responsible to us in like manner as
aforesaid.

5. The guardian, moreover, so long as he has the
wardship of the land, shall keep up the houses,
parks, fish ponds, stanks, mills, and other things
pertaining to the land, out of the issues of the same
land; and he shall restore to the heir, when he has
come to full age, all his land, stocked with ploughs
and "waynage," according as the season of
husbandry shall require, and the issues of the land
can reasonably bear.

6. Heirs shall be married without disparagement,
yet so that before the marriage takes place the
nearest in blood to that heir shall have notice.

7. A widow, after the death of her husband, shall

forthwith and without difficulty have her marriage portion and inheritance; nor shall she give anything for her dower, or for her marriage portion, or for the inheritance which her husband and she held on the day of the death of that husband; and she may remain in the house of her husband for fourty days after his death, within which time her dower shall be assigned to her.

8. No widow shall be compelled to marry, so long as she prefers to live without a husband; provided always that she gives security not to marry without our consent, if she holds of us, or without the consent of the lord of whom she holds, if she holds of another.

9. Neither we nor our bailiffs shall seize any land or rent for any debt, so long as the chattels of the debtor are sufficient to repay the debt; nor shall the sureties of the debtor be distrained so long as the principal debtor is able to satisfy the debt; and if the principal debtor shall fail to pay the debt, having nothing wherewith to pay it, then the sureties shall answer for the debt; and let them have the lands and rents of the debtor, if they desire them, until they are indemnified for the debt which they have paid for him, unless the principal debtor can show proof that he is discharged thereof as against the said sureties.

10. If one who has borrowed from the Jews any sum, great or small, die before that loan can be repaid, the debt shall not bear interest while the heir is under age, of whomsoever he may hold; and if the debt fall into our hands, we will not take anything except the principal sum contained in the bond.

11. And if any one die indebted to the Jews, his wife shall have her dower and pay nothing of that debt; and if any children of the deceased are left under age, necessaries shall be provided for them in keeping with the holding of the deceased; and out of the residue the debt shall be paid, reserving, however, service due to feudal lords; in like manner let it be done touching debts due to others than Jews.

12. No scutage nor aid shall be imposed on our kingdom, unless by common counsel of our kingdom, except for ransoming our person, for making our eldest son a knight, and for once marrying our eldest daughter; and for these there shall not be levied more than a reasonable aid. In like manner it shall be done concerning aids from the city of London.

13. And the city of London shall have all its ancient liberties and free customs, as well by land as by water; furthermore, we decree and grant that all

other cities, boroughs, towns, and ports shall have all their liberties and free customs.

14. And for obtaining the common counsel of the kingdom anent the assessing of an aid (except in the three cases afore said) or of a scutage, we will cause to be summoned the archbishops, bishops, abbots, earls, and greater barons, severally by our letters; and we will moreover cause to be summoned generally, through our sheriffs and bailiffs, all others who hold of us in chief, for afixed date, namely, after the expiry of at least forty days, and at a fixed place; and in all letters of such summons we will specify the reason of the summons. And when the summons has thus been made, the business shall proceed on the day appointed, according to the counsel of such as are present, although not all who were summoned have come.

15. We will not for the future grant to any one license to take an aid from his own free tenants, except to ransom his body, to make his eldest son a knight, and once to marry his eldest daughter; and on each of these occasions there shall be levied only a reasonable aid.

16. No one shall be distrained for performance of greater service for aknight's fee, or for any other free tenement, than is due therefrom.

17. Common pleas shall not follow our court, but shall be held in some fixed place.

18. Inquests of novel disseisin, ofmort d'ancester, and of darrein presentment, shall not be held elsewhere than in their own county courts and that in manner following,--We, or, if we should be out of the realm, our chief justiciar, will send two justiciars through every county four times a year, who shall, along with four knights of the county chosen by the county, hold the said assize in the county court, on the day and in the place of meeting of that court.

19. And if any of the said assizes cannot be taken on the day of the county court, let there remain of the knights and free holders, who were present at the county court on that day, as many as may be required for the efficient making of judgments, according as the business be more or less.

20. A freeman shall not be amerced for a slight offense, except in accordance with the degree of the offense; and for a grave offense he shall be amerced in accordance with the gravity of the offense, yet saving always his"contenement;" and a merchant in the same way, saving his "merchandise;" and a villein shall be amerced in the same way, saving his "wainage"--if they have fallen into our mercy: and none of the aforesaid amercements shall be impsed

except by the oath of honest men of the neigh-
borhood.

21. Earls and barons shall not be amerced except
through their peers, and only in accordance with the
degree of the offense.

22. A clerk shall not be amerced in respect of his
lay holding except after the manner of the others
aforesaid; further, he shall not be amerced in accordance with the extent of his ecclesiastical benefice.

23. No village or individual shall be compelled to
make bridges atriver-banks, except those who from
of old were legally bound to do so.

24. No sheriff, constable, coroners, or others of
our bailiffs, shall hold pleas of our Crown.

25. All counties, hundreds, wapentakes, and
trithings (except our demesnemanors) shall remain
at old rents, and without any additional payment.

26. If any one holding of us a lay fief shall die,
and our sheriff or bailiff shall exhibit our letters
patent of summons for a debt which the deceased
owed to us, it shall be lawful for our sheriff or bailiff
to attach and catalogue chattels of the deceased,
found upon the lay fief, to the value of that debt, at
the sight of law-worthy men, provided always that
nothing whatever be thence removed until the debt
which is evident shall be fully paid to us; and the

residue shall be left to the executors to fulfil the will of the deceased; and if there be nothing due from him to us, all the chattels shall go to the deceased, saving to his wife and children their reasonable shares.

27. If any freeman shall die intestate, his chattels shall be distributed bythe hands of his nearest kins-folk and friends, under supervision of the church, saving to every one the debts which the deceased owed to him.

28. No constable or other bailiff of ours shall take corn or other provisions from any one without immediately tendering money therefor, unless he can have postponement thereof by permission of the seller.

29. No constable shall compel any knight to give money in lieu of castle-guard, when he is willing to perform it in his own person, or (if hecannot do it from any reasonable cause) then by another respon-sible man. Further, if we have led or sent him upon military service, he shall be relieved from guard in proportion to the time during which he has been on servicebecause of us.

30. No sheriff or bailiff of ours, or other person, shall take the horses or carts of any freeman for transport duty, against the will of the said freeman.

31. Neither we nor our bailiffs shall take, for our castles or for any other work of ours, wood which is not ours, against the will of the owner of that wood.

32. We will not retain beyond one year and one day, the lands of those who have been convicted of felony, and the lands shall thereafter be handed over to the lords of the fiefs.

33. All kiddles for the future shall be removed altogether from Thames and Medway, and throughout all England, except upon the seashore.

34. The writ which is called praecipe shall not for the future be issued to any one, regarding any tenement whereby a freeman may lose hiscourt.

35. Let there be one measure of wine throughout our whole realm; and one measure of ale; and one measure of corn, to wit, "the London quarter;" and one width of cloth (whether dyed, or russet, or "halberget"), to wit, two ells within the selvages; of weights also let it be as of measures.

36. Nothing in future shall be given or taken for a writ of inquisition of life or limbs, but freely it shall be granted, and never denied.

37. If any one holds of us by fee-farm, by socage, or by burgage, and holds also land of another lord by knight's service, we will not (by reason of thatfee-farm, socage, or burgage) have the wardship of the

heir, or of such land of his as is of the fief of that other; nor shall we have wardship of that fee-farm, socage, or burgage, unless such fee-farm owes knight's service. We will not by reason of any small serjeanty which any one may hold of us by the service of rendering to us knives, arrows, or the like, have wardship of his heir of of the land which he holds of another lord by knight's service.

38. No bailiff for the future shall, upon his own unsupported complaint, putany one to his "law," without credible witnesses brought for this purpose.

39. No freeman shall be taken or imprisoned or disseised or exiled or in anyway destroyed, nor will we go upon him nor send upon him, except by the lawful judgment of his peers or by the law of the land.

40. To no one will we sell, to no one will we refuse or delay, right or justice.

41. All merchants shall have safe and secure exit from England, and entry to England, with the right to tarry there and to move about as well by land as bywater, for buying and selling by the ancient and right customs, quit from allevil tolls, except (in time of war) such merchants as are of the land at warwith us. And if such are found in our land at the beginning of the war, they shall be deltained, without

injury to their bodies or goods, until information be received by us, or by our chief justiciar, how the merchants of our land found in the land at war with us are treated; and if our men are safe there, the others shall be safe in our land.

42. It shall be lawful in future for any one (excepting always those imprisoned or outlawed in accordance with the law of the kingdom, and natives of any country at war with us, and merchants, who shall be treated as is above provided) to leave our kingdom and to return, safe and secure by land and water, except for a short period in time of war, on grounds of public policy--reserving always the allegiance due to us.

43. If any one holding of some escheat (such as the honor of Wallingford, Nottingham, Boulogne, Lancaster, or of other escheats which are in our handsand are baronies) shall die, his heir shall give no other relief, and perform no other service to us than he would have done to the baron, if that barony had been in the baron's hand; and we shall hold it in the same manner in which the baron held it.

44. Men who dwell without the forest need not henceforth come before our justiciars of the forest upon a general summons, except those who are

impleaded, or who have become sureties for any person or persons attached for forest offenses.

45. We will appoint as justices, constables, sheriffs, or bailiffs only such as know the law of the realm and mean to observe it well.

46. All barons who have founded abbeys, concerning which they hold charters from the kings of England, or of which they have long-continued possession, shall have the wardship of them, when vacant, as they ought to have.

47. All forests that have been made such in our time shall forthwith be disafforested; and a similar course shall be followed with regard to river-banks that have been placed "in defense" by us in our time.

48. All evil customs connected with forests and warrens, foresters and warreners, sheriffs and their officers, river-banks and their wardens, shall immediately be inquired into in each county by twelve sworn knights of the same county chosen by the honest men of the same county, and shall, within forty days of the said inquest, be utterly abolished, so as never to be restored, provided always that we previously have intimation thereof, or our justiciar, if we should not be in England.

49. We will immediately restore all hostages and

charters delivered to us by Englishmen, as sureties of the peace or of faithful service.

50. We will entirely remove from their bailiwicks, the relations of Gerard Athee (so that in future they shall have no bailiwick in England); namely, Engelard of Cigogne, Peter, Guy, and Andrew of Chanceaux, Guy of Cigogne, Geofrrey of Martigny with his brothers, Philip Mark with his brothers and his nephew Geoffrey, and the whole brood of the same.

51. As soon as peace is restored, we will banish from the kingdom all foreign-born knights, crossbowmen, serjeants, and mercenary soldiers, who have come with horses and arms to the kingdom's hurt.

52. If any one has been dispossessed or removed by us, without the legal judgment of his peers, from his lands, castles, franchises, or from his right, we will immediately restore them to him; and if a dispute arise over this, then let it be decided by the five-and-twenty barons of whom mention is made below in the clause for securing the peace. Moreover, for all those possessions,from which any one has, without the lawful judgment of his peers, been disseised or removed, by our father, King Henry, or by our brother, King Richard, and which we retain in

our hand (or which are possessed by others, to whom we are bound to warrant them) we shall have respite until the usual term of crusaders; excepting those things about which a plea has been raised, or an inquest made by our order, before our taking of the cross; but as soon as we return from our expedition (or if perchance we desist from the expedition) we will immediately grant full justice therein.

53. We shall have, moreover, the same respite and in the same manner in rendering justice concerning the disafforestation or retention of those forests which Henry our father and Richard our brother afforested, and concerning wardship of lands which are of the fief of another (namely, such wardships as we have hitherto had by reason of a fief which any one held of us by knight's service), and concerning abbeys founded on other fiefs than our own, in which the lord of the fief claims to have right; and when we have returned, or if we desist from our expedition, we will immediately grant full justice to all who complain of such things.

54. No one shall be arrested or imprisoned upon the appeal of a woman, for the death of any other than her husband.

55. All fines made with us unjustly and against

the law of the land, and all amercements imposed unjustly and against the law of the land, shall be entirely remitted, or else it shall be done concerning them according to the decision of the five-and-twenty barons of whom mention is made below in the clause for securing the peace, or according to the judgment of the majority of the same, along with the aforesaid Stephen, archbishop of Canterbury, if he can be present, and such others as he may wish to bring with him for this purpose, and if he cannot be present the business shall nevertheless proceed without him, provided always that if any one or more of the aforesaid five-and-twenty barons are in a similar suit, they shall be removed as far as concerns this particular judgment, others being substituted in their places after having been selected by the rest of the same five-and-twenty for this purpose only, and after having been sworn.

56. If we have disseised or removed Welshmen from lands or liberties, or other things, without the legal judgment of their peers in England or in Wales, they shall be immediately restored to them; and if a dispute arise over this, then let it be decided in the marches by the judgment of their peers; for tenements in England according to the law of England,

for tenements in Wales according to the law of Wales, and for tenements in the marches according to the law of the marches. Welshmen shall do the same to us and ours.

57. Further, for all those possessions from which any Welshman has, without the lawful judgment of his peers, been disseised or removed by King Henry our father or King Richard our brother, and which we retain in our hand (or which are possessed by others, to whom we are bound to warrant them) we shall have respite until the usual term of crusaders; excepting those things about which a plea has been raised or an inquest made by our order before we took the cross; but as soon as we return (or if perchance we desist from our expedition), we will immediately grant full justice in accordance with the laws of the Welsh and in relation to the foresaid regions.

58. We will immediately give up the son of Llywelyn and all the hostages of Wales, and the charters delivered to us as security for the peace.

59. We will do toward Alexander, King of Scots, concerning the return of his sisters and his hostages, and concerning his franchises, and his right, in the same manner as we shall do toward our other barons of England, unless it ought to be otherwise

according to the charters which we hold from William his father, formerly King of Scots; and this shall be according to the judgment of his peers in our court.

60. Moreover, all these aforesaid customs and liberties, the observance of which we have granted in our kingdom as far as pertains to us toward our men, shall be observed by all of our kingdom, as well clergy as laymen, as far as pertains to them toward their men.

61. Since, moreover, for God and the amendment of our kingdom and for the better allaying of the quarrel that has arisen between us and our barons, we have granted all these concessions, desirous that they should enjoy them incomplete and firm endurance for ever, we give and grant to them the underwritten security, namely, that the barons choose five-and-twenty barons of the kingdom, whomsoever they will, who shall be bound with all their might, to observe and hold, and cause to be observed, the peace and liberties we have granted and confirmed to them by this our present Charter, so that if we, or our justiciar, or our bailiffs or any one of our officers, shall in anything beat fault toward any one, or shall have broken any one of the articles of the peace or of this security, and the

offense be notified to four barons of the foresaid five-and-twenty, the said four barons shall repair to us (or our justiciar, if we are out of the realm) and, laying the transgression before us, petition to have that transgression redressed without delay. And if we shall not have corrected the transgression (or, in the event of our being out of the realm, if our justiciar shall not have corrected it) within forty days, reckoning from the time it has been intimated to us (or to our justiciar, if we should be out of the realm), the four barons aforesaid shall refer that matter to the rest of the five-and-twenty barons, and those five-and-twenty barons shall, together with the community of the whole land, distrain and distress us in all possible ways, namely, by seizing our castles, lands, possessions, and in any other way they can, until redress has been obtained as they deem fit, saving harmless our own person, and the persons of our queen and children; and when redress has been obtained, they shall resume their old relations toward us. And let whoever in the country desires it, swear to obey the orders of the said five-and-twenty barons for the execution of all the aforesaid matters, and along with them, to molest us to the utmost of his power; and we publicly and freely grant leave to every one who wishes to swear, and we shall never forbid any one to swear. All those, moreover, in the land who of themselves and of their own accord are unwilling to swear to the twenty-five to help them inconstraining and molesting us, we shall by our command compel the same to swear to the effect aforesaid. And if any one of the five-and-twenty barons shall have died or departed from the land, or be incapacitated in any other manner which would prevent the foresaid provisions being carried out, those of the said twenty-five barons who are left shall choose another in his place according to their own judgment, and he shall be sworn in the same way as the others. Further, in all matters, the execution of which is intrusted to these twenty-five barons, if perchance these twenty-five are present, that which the majority of those present ordain or command shall be held as fixed and established, exactly as if the whole twenty-five had concurred in this; and the said twenty-five shall swear that they will faithfully observe all that is aforesaid, and cause it to be observed with all their might. And we shall procure nothing from any one, directly or indirectly, whereby any part of these concessions and liberties might be revoked or diminished; and if any such thing has been procured, let it be void and null, and we shall never use it personally or by another.

62. And all the ill-will, hatreds, and bitterness that have arisen between us and our men, clergy and lay, from the date of the quarrel, we have completely remitted and pardoned every one. Moreover, all trespasses occasioned by the said quarrel, from Easter in the sixteenth year of our reign till the restoration of peace, we have fully remitted to all, both clergy and laymen, and completely forgiven, as far as pertains to us. And, on this head, we have caused to be made for them letters testimonial patent of the lord Stephen, archbishop of Canterbury, of the lord Henry, archbishop of Dublin, of the bishops aforesaid, and of Master Pandulf as touching this security and the concessions aforesaid.

63. Wherefore it is our will, and we firmly enjoin, that the English Church be free, and that the men in our kingdom have and hold all the aforesaid liberties, rights, and concessions, well and peaceably, freely and quietly, fully and wholly, for themselves and their heirs, of us and our heirs, in all respects and in all places for ever, as is aforesaid. An oath, moreover, has been taken, as well on our part as on the part of the barons, that all these conditions aforesaid shall be kept in good faith and without evil intent. Given under our hand--the above-named and many others being witnesses--in the meadow which

is called Runnymede, between Windsor and Staines, on the fifteenth day of June, in the seventeenth year of our reign.